High on Table Mountain

High on Table Mountain

Poems

Elizabeth Weir

NORTH STAR PRESS OF ST. CLOUD, INC.
St. Cloud, Minnesota

ISBN: 978-1-68201-019-8

Printed in the United States of America.

Published by
North Star Press of St. Cloud, Inc.
St. Cloud, MN

www.northstarpress.com
www.elizabethvweir.com

For my family on both sides of the Atlantic

Acknowledgements

I am particularly grateful to North Star Press for their guidance and support in publishing my first book of poetry.

I wish to thank Intermedia Arts and the Jerome Foundation, sponsors of the SASE: the Write Place mentorship programs that gave me opportunities to study with poets John Caddy, Richard Reichard, Todd Boss, and Deborah Keenan, each of whom has been invaluable in guiding me along the path of poetry to the destination of *High on Table Mountain*.

It began at Normandale Community College, where Professor Chet Corey took an interest in my writing. At Metropolitan State University, Professors Piers and Kathy Lewis and Lawrence Moe, and Professor Deborah Keenan from Hamline University encouraged me to write. I thank the Loft Literary Center, and poet and friend Phyllis Katz, who introduced me to the Frost Place in New Hampshire, which I was fortunate to attend twice.

Just as essential to my writing are my two poetry groups, with Todd Boss, Sharon Chmielarz, Dore Kiesselbach, and Tim Nolan, and with Teresa Boyer, Kirsten Dierking, Ann Iverson, Janet Jerve, Kathy Weihe, Marie Rickmyer, and Tracy Youngblom-Turner. Along the way, poets Diane Frank and Carolyn Bell, and writers Susan Hamre, Erin Hart, Lynda McDonell, Cheryll Ostrom, and Claudia Poser have critiqued my work. Invaluable, with his close editorial eye, is my husband, Ken.

Credits

I wish to thank the following publications in which these poems have appeared, some under different titles:

Comstock Review, "I Always Eat an Apple Whole;" "Late News from my Grandfather, Percival Vincent Fright."

White Pelican Review, "Casuarina Trees Feather Against Moonlight;" "How Sweet the Silence of Lemons."

Water~Stone Review, "Lamb."

Sidewalks, "Long Fingers of Early Light;" "Where She Hid;" "A Leopard Frog Swirls;" "Your Midnight Bed."

Beloved of the Earth; 150 poems of Grief and Gratitude, a Holy Cow! Press Anthology, "The Smell of Apples."

Alimentum, "Chutney."

ArtWord Quarterly, "Secret;" "Impact."

Main Channel Voices, "Libation;" "Two Snakes Twined in Bridal Veil;" "You've Got to Love a Man who Cares Enough to Stop and Kill;" "At Gate 38 C, Denver Airport;" "Suddenly Swans;" "Negative Form;" "Kitchen Alchemy;" "The Things They Love but No Longer Need;" "Leaving for America;" "The Daily Smallness of Being;" "On Tiptoe, I Listen."

Flurry, "The Touch of Time."

Mother Superior, "Winter Blends, A Lyric."

Out of Line, "Pointe du Hoc, Normandy;" "Terezin;" "I Cut a White Onion."

Second Wind, "The Snap of The Unseen."

Turtle Lit, "She Slices Soft Pears;" "To an Unpracticed Eye."

The Heart of All That Is: Reflections on Home, a Holy Cow! Press Anthology, "Thoughts Upon Returning Home to an English Spring."

Contents

Section III
The Waxing Three-Quarter Moon

Section IV
The Full Moon

Section V
The Waning Quarter Moon

Section VI
The Fading Crescent Moon

"As the phases of the moon trace a lunar cycle,
so this work traces the arc of a life."
~E.W.

High on Table Mountain
Friends Meet After Thirty-seven Years

We sip Oyster Bay sauvignon blanc
and our palates become terraced vineyards,
sun-drenched and rain-washed,
bee hum and tendril climb.

Aged roots draw up lost youth
from the dry gravel of years—

wind-swished hair in an open TR 5,
pine-warm picnics high on Table Mountain;
tender English skins blister,
then burnish brown beneath Africa's sun,
us, nursing the sick, off-duty flirting,
satin nights, hot with possibility,
our eyes, soft with knowledge,
hips locked to Simon and Garfunkel.

"To then," toasts David. Six stemmed glasses
clink, and Helios arcs his fiery chariot
across the absent years, leans down,
ripples fingertips through molten time.

Section I

The Young Crescent Moon

"The night walked down the sky with the moon in her hand."
~Frederic Lawrence Knowles

Casuarina Trees Feather Against Moonlight

We search for Alpha and Beta Centauri,
unfamiliar stars in a Southern sky, listen,
as beneath our feet, the luminous sea
sucks and chuckles at jetty pilings.

The beaten silver surface breaches—
we hear a primal in-draw of breath.
Then quiet. Triangular ray wings
stroke the current and glide into darkness.

A lone sand shark sinews past;
a deep sigh, and a loggerhead turtle
rocks on sea sway, massive shell
bumping wood, nose pointed up at us.

Eyes meet and linger.
The turtle submerges, flippers
surging into the moon's brimming path.
We loose it in radiance and long to

dive down, into silken waters,
among fins and purple coral fans,
down, into each other,
to rise in phosphorescent fire.

Reading *Paradise Lost* by Candlelight

No power tonight. I strike a match
and light a candle end in an old pewter stick.
Perhaps, just such a flame cast light
on the quill of blind Milton's daughter,
as he dictated his epic of a paradise
dull in its endless perfection. Her quill
must have slowed in the thrown light
when still-innocent Eve and docile Adam
filled her father's thoughts.

But when Satan and his mob
thronged in the great void,
when he slithered into Eden
and tempted Eve to pluck
the succulent apple,
then his daughter's pen quickened—
how Milton's words tumbled
across the foolscap, bright
as new-minted brass farthings,
words fleet with iniquity to beguile
readers as fallen as God's dark angel.

She Slices Soft Pears

cored boats, wet in hand,
slips a sliver between her lips,

stops to stir her reduction—
port wine, a cut of butter,

two spoons of apple juice,
a pour of honey.

White raisins plump
in hot bubble, he waiting.

She shakes in cardamom
and cinnamon, kitchen still,

candles lit, folds pears,
into her thickening happiness,

dips in her wooden spoon;
tastes her readiness.

Long Fingers of Early Light

touch pale pears swelling with summer.
I sit, heavy, on the top stoop step
to admire my dawn endeavors:
weed-free in fresh-turned earth,
cream and brick-red freesias bloom.

Since first light, I have ripped
vagrant plants from their chosen root,
denying them their chance to seed.
Now, in heating sun, I wilt
like chickweed, limp at my feet.

My swollen fruit stirs with life.
Through thin cotton, I hold
my globed abdōmen. Beneath
my earthy palms, our first child's
budding limbs unfurl.

Chutney

Dice three pounds of firm green tomatoes,
six apples and one large yellow onion. Ladle in

two cups of cider vinegar for sharpness,
two cups of brown sugar for sweetness,

three teaspoons of mixed spices for zeal. Add
five crushed garlic cloves and half a cup

of fresh-grated root ginger to make it kick.
Shake in whole coriander seeds to entice the tongue

with hints of citron, the dust and silks of India.
Set the pot to simmer for one hour. Never forget

the raisins, handfuls of golden raisins, sweet and tart,
plumped with rain and sun. Stir at intervals.

Boil jars and lids separately. On a whim, toss in
slivered almonds. Taste a lick, and if it fills

your head with autumn, the argy-bargy of brothers
romping upstairs and your mother's raised voice,

spoon it, two scoops per jar and screw
the lids on tight. Sponge down glass

with hot water to clean off sticky runnels
and set aside to cool. If your kitchen

stays silent, it's a bad sign. But if the air
clicks with the sounds of sealing

stick on labels, date and title "Chutney."
                    Now, sign your name.

Lamb
England, February, 1947

Our feet crunch on a thin crust of snow in Nonsuch Park.
"Strange," says Daddy, "this snow in February."
He holds Mummy's arm, says she must not to slip. Ahead,
a huddle of sheep shelters in a copse out of the keen wind.
An old man, dressed in grubby sweaters, kneels beside a sheep—

a rope of blood hangs from her bottom! She cries and cries,
each cry written in a puff of mist, like in my brothers' comics.
A crumpled heap steams at the man's knees.
"That's a mother sheep," Daddy says. "Her baby's dead.
Let's see how the shepherd will help her."

"Mornin'," the old man nods at my father. He pulls a knife
from a cloth roll and turns the dead lamb onto its back.
Mummy presses my face into her red coat, against the tight
ball of her stomach. Daddy says, "Let her watch, my dear."
As the shepherd slits from chin to belly,

thin skin curls away from the knife's cut. Mummy holds
her tummy, turns away, and Daddy puts his arm around her.
The man cuts down the back of each leg, around hooves,
black as coal chips, up the tail and across the head. He peels
the fur off the lamb, like I pull the coat off my dress-up doll.

I reach for Daddy's hand. The sheep bleats for her dead baby.
The shepherd pulls a tangle of twine from a torn pocket,
eases through his flock, talking to each sheep, and scoops up
the smallest lamb of a mother with three. "Born in the night,"
he calls to my father. "Do better wi' a milk bag of 'is own."

He knots the dead lamb's skin onto its back, stretches
it over head and bottom and gives the wrapped lamb to the sheep.
She sniffs, bangs it with her head and cries for her own baby.
The old man rubs his hands in dead lamb blood, wipes them
over the string-tied skin and gives the lamb back to the sheep.

She smells it. Pushes it with her nose. Sniffs again and licks the skin.
"She'll take," the shepherd nods to Daddy. "They all do."
"It's true," Mummy sighs, gloved hands cradling her tummy.
"We all take. We can't help it." The sheep is quiet.
She has her lamb. He drinks her milk and wags his double tail.

Upon Returning Home to an English Spring
After Jim Moore

Mists of cow parsley massed under chestnuts
smell as immediate as childhood—

no one knows how to love the way I do
the scent of syringa outside my girlhood window;
the wag in our dog's bottom when we pedal home
from school; our mother's voice irritable
from the constant scrimp and save of life;
our kitchen warm with the promise of baked jam tarts;
the black-silk feel of Trevor's tea-drinking rabbit,
as he laps from my brother's china saucer;
little Nicky, clamoring to tell an endless story;
us arguing, loud and daft, over who reads
the *Beano* comic first; Mummy relaxing in the curl
of her after-tea cigarette and our quiet dad,
wreathed in clouds of worry about money.

Me, climbing the stairs and loving the feeling
of falling asleep in the scratch and wrap of family,
Danny, the cat, snugged tight in the crook of my knees.

Tea Dust and Tarnish

His spoon's yellowed bowl flares like a sea scallop shell,
stubby handle, balanced. My father scooped
loose tea, smoky as old rope, one spoon for each person
and one for the pot; he liked his tea strong and hot,
three minutes beneath the cozy to steep, then pour.
With his brass spoon, I scoop a heaping of Darjeeling
into my kitchen teapot. I like a weaker brew.

Winter warmth comes skimming down a sun shaft.
I remember the Easter morning I awoke to my father
clucking and flapping hen elbows on my bed.
On my Paisley eiderdown, he laid a golden-wrapped
chocolate Easter egg—still warm to my touch!
I kept that egg, in its foil, for years, unable to eat
anything that could come from such a place.

My handsome father whose large ears embarrassed me
when I brought home friends from school, my gentle father
whom my mother wanted to be an ambitious man,
my father, who walked to see the sun set twice,
once from a hollow, then from a high place.
On impulse, I find Silvo and a rag. His spoon shines
with the soft patina that wear and time bring to fine silver.

Fins into Wind

Bullfish fins ripple in the lapping lake.
A low-slung cormorant swims above, flips
under, corks up, bullfish locked in hooked bill.
Black fish muscle thrashes.

The bird slaps its catch on water skin.
Bullfish torques its dorsal fin, curls
its tail in spasm. Gape of yellow bill
and fish tail flashes—gone.

Throat plumage rolls over fish squirm
in the feathered churn of the swollen gullet.
A sudden skitter. Wings and feet batter
fractured water, until bird and fish lift

into mutability, scales into feathers, fins
into wind, the ordinary into suddenness—
the normal, unhinged
from the deep knowing of what is.

Section II

The Growing Quarter Moon

"I like to think the moon is there, even when
I am not looking at it."
~Albert Einstein

A Lament for My Father

I picture the long coffin for my tall father,
six men, dressed in Dickens-black,
waxen gladioli in stiff arrangements
and me, not there.

I picture my family gathered in England,
our first great loss. Mother,
brave but blanched as marble,
and me, not beside her.

I picture bearers setting his coffin,
on a tray of pale trumpet lilies,
straightening its drape of tired purple,
and me, imagining . . .

I picture my eldest brother speaking,
"Let us honor the life of Charles Pearman . . ."
the choke in his voice barely checked,
and me, in silence.

I picture all rise to sing, guess at the hum
of an unseen conveyor as it glides
our dear Father into our pasts,
and me, apart,

here, on the far toe of Africa,
our just-born baby in my arms.
I hold him close,
cannot let go.

Leaving for America

I pack long underwear for extreme cold,
skirts, boots and woolen jumpers, sandals
and Indian cotton for summer heat,
Lego for the boys and favorite books,
A.A. Milne for them, Jane Austen for me.
In soft cottons, I wrap binoculars, fit in a guide
to the common birds of North America,
photos of my mother, brothers and sisters-in-law.
I tuck in the sounds of village cricket, willow bat
striking leather ball on Oxted's tended green,
the joyful yelps of small cousins, chasing around
my brother's rose beds. Christopher tittering
at his own jokes, the song-thrush on the roof peak
singing to a close this life I know. I pack
my mother's voice, our stomach-sadness,
bundle it tight, stuff it in. Shut the lid.
Mark the case, "FRAGILE."

Six Sober Months of Winter in Frozen Minnesota

The children and I, bottled up indoors.
Short sorties to romp and slide in snow
before fifteen degrees below zero forces retreat.

My stoppered longing for home and family
lies buried beneath two-foot drifts of stoicism.
Then, one morning, I step outside into air

heady as Champagne. Soft slush underfoot,
our maple, a chartreuse burst of florets.
Two young apricots stand sleeved in cream

the color of Bailey's Irish. I look around.
A single maple in the woods blooms rosé,
luminous as new wine. I reel and totter,

giddy on an unexpected swig of spring.

Winter Blends, a Lyric

Snow veils the windows
of a Minnesota afternoon,
as we sit around the embers
of a maple-log fire and sip
the harvest of the Orient,
Lapsang, Ceylon, Assam, Oolong.

Finland, Chile, India, England—
accents blend like the teas we sip
from peacock-painted china cups.
In the silver-bellied teapot
steeps long-leaved Darjeeling,
Keemun, Luk-on, Pu-li, Soushong.

Our children play at our feet and speak
in accents grown unlike our own. We know
we must adapt but cling to past traditions,
tea, finger sandwiches, scones and cream,
the ache of doubleness in our bones,
Lapsang, Ceylon, Assam, Oolong.

Libation

O.E.D.: pouring of wine to honor a god

Raspberries grow few and tight
among stricken vines
on drought-stunned bushes,
their taste, intense as raisins.

If I were an Ibo elder, I would slit
the throat of a cock, grasp his legs
and spatter pulsing blood on parched
earth to placate capricious gods.

I stand to stretch my back and see
a cloud of silent pelicans. Stately
as airships, holy birds slow-wheel
beneath a tungsten sky, as though

they have always sailed there, as though
they bear gifts from distant time.
Black-pinioned wings hold still,
merely dip to bend the circled air.

Heads hunch between white shoulders,
heavy bills glow orange in gray light.
I hail these ancient water birds
and watch as they kettle higher, drift

and slide southward, beyond
the tree line, and a plump drop of rain,
ripe as plenty, plunks
on my glasses. More drops, until

I am wrapped in rain. I spread
my arms, spin and spin in wetness,
spill drought-sweet raspberries,
scarlet on thirsty earth.

A Leopard Frog Swirls

limbs splayed, in the chlorinated water of a pool.
I ease toward it, raise my hand, slow as a displaced
lily pad that glides to the surface after a canoe's passing,
until the frog rests, contented, on my outstretched palm.

Its enameled skin gleams iridescent in sunlight.
Black spots line its lithe back, slide over tented hips,
fold into stripes along its muscled thighs.
High eyes are two bronze beads, slit with obsidian.

I raise my other hand and cup the frog. Down the hill
I hurry. The slippery frog squirms and shoves against
the trap of my hands. At lake's edge, I unlock my fingers:
the frog kicks free and splashes into familiarity. Envy

floods my ventricles; I look across the lake, across
half a continent and the Atlantic to a crowded land
of low skies, family jokes and my brothers' laughter,
old anecdotes, to England, where I know how to belong.

In the Hug of Night
After Eavan Boland

Friends have left and I am glad.
The sleeping house draws in close;
I count the hall clock's eleven chimes
and let day slide from me.

Wine glasses dry in the rack,
dishwasher pumping its wet music,
furnace sighing hushed warmth—
quiet, domestic and intimate.

On the kitchen table,
an olive-green mug,
cocoa crusting its rim,
teaspoon puddled beside it.

A thump above—Conor's book
dropped from drowsy fingers.
In the woodstove's warm belly,
embers cave and settle.

Time is a drip, a tock, a shift.
I slip into the arms of night
and leave the spoon and mug
complicit in spilled chocolate.

Kitchen Alchemy

I set my wooden spoon to dance among onions
and admire the way its busy hips
flare into the shallow belly of its bowl.
This spoon and I wear the mark of common years.
Together, we have braised kilos of raw beef,
basket-loads of mushrooms, whole fields of onions.
We are nicked and stained with the soil
of constant cooking. We stir full-bodied
Burgundy into red currant sauce.
We spike dull gravies with rum and sherry.
Our horseradish makes a cool cucumber hot.
Chili gingers our fibers. We bind
butter and eggs into velvet Béarnaise.
At our touch, a custard thickens,
pea pods glisten bright green.
Raw chicken turns gold.
We make the tough, tender,
we change skinny boys into men,
we keep a man constant—sorcery
in our seasoned bowls.

The Things They Love But No Longer Need

The youngest went first. In his room
Conor left lake-bleached wood, labeled fossils,
a lamp with photos of friends pinned to its shade.

The day he moved, we quarreled over which mattress
should be taken, which left behind;
the real issue, not the mattress.

Fergus leaked away by degrees. For weeks
he sorted and tossed out boyhood posters,
grade-school papers, broken trophies.

Tonight, both boys are home. We sit around
the kitchen table, laugh and chat over roast lamb
and plum crumble, just like always.

At the door, we wave goodbye.
Our children are visitors. We watch their tail-lights
fade into September dark.

The Touch of Time

He wears a yellow scarf and a red bucket fez.
Charcoal chunks curve in a smile; jaunty nose, a corner
of broken brick. His black bung eyes shine in morning sun,
twig arms uplifted, one mittened in gray, one in pink.

He wears time like a worn-out jacket. Doubt
settles in every crystal. Teeth scatter at his feet; he lists
towards uncertainty. Red fez falls. One stick arm slips
from its socket, the other gestures to a vacant sky.

Section III

The Waxing Three-Quarter Moon

"We are all like the bright moon;
we still have our darker side."
~Khalil Gibran

Fighting an Unstable Line

I grapple shirts and sheets in hot wind and do not hear
her car arrive. She says, *We've got to talk,* and
blue shirt sleeves entangle me in a damp embrace.

Help me hang the wash first. *I'm pregnant,*
she blurts. A sheet billows, biffing me off balance.
She will keep the pregnancy, too late for choice,

keep her baby. I understand. Pretty girl,
clever, but unable to care for a pet;
she lost her cat. Her college room,

a chaos of dirty clothes, dried cat turds
and scattered litter. Our son's fury frightens her.
Chill tightens my chest. I cannot talk,

cannot think. Go, I beg. Forgive me, but go.
I'll call you—later. I leave unpegged pillowcases
and heavy towels in the spilling basket, fearful

the line might break under the strain.

Secret

A black snake
sinuous as shame
eyes
a knee-high
chink in
the corner
of our brick house.
You watch it
rear, stretch
and
slap back on stone.
It re-coils
its length,
muscles itself
sideways
on rough mortar,
slithers up
and slides
in.

You know
it must come out
some day.
You won't know
where. You
won't know
when.

You
hurry inside,
shut
the front door,
and shove home
the bolt.

Unbidden

you come among hushed anger.
Your birth numbs two stunned families, you,
knowing only the urgency of milk, the comfort
of warmth. Your father knows you as an expense,
your grandfather, locked in pained silence.

Your Iowa grandparents fold you
into their days. I edge between discretion
and despair and keep in touch by telephone.

Your other grandma invites me to visit. At her door,
I meet an eighteen-month-old with my son's eyes.
You lift hands, square and familiar; you point,
say, "Wiz," as though you have always known me.

Scattered Sunlight

I

A bottle-green dragonfly darts over fresh-mown lawn.
Black-daubed wings scatter sunlight, legs bunch
to basket mosquitoes. It hovers in a shimmer of heat,
a precise flyer, designed for sleek air. A burn
of citrus and chestnut and a great-crested flycatcher
snatches the dragonfly on the wing and lands in the ash.
The bird anchors the squirming insect, plucks
four polished wing-panes that flicker as they fall.
Dark body in beak, the flycatcher swoops
deep into shadowed woods.

II

I amble through sun-steeped prairie. Bee balm
and wild indigo bloom. A sulphur-wing butterfly
probes a spire of purple gayfeather. Prairie roses blow
pink among yellow drop-seed. A breeze
lofts my hair, and, somewhere, a dicsissal sings.
My cell phone chimes the opening bars of Bach's
"Toccata and Fugue in D Minor." It's my grandson's stepfather:
"You," he fumes, "are banished from seeing Peter."
The claw of his anger pierces me.
The line goes dead. I plunge into darkness.

Negative Form
On Our Grandson Being Gone

In a squirrel scrape in winter woods
beneath granular snow, beneath leaves
matted by frost, down in the frozen earth,
I find the perfect absence of an acorn.

Precise clay records the scar
of the stem that fed the acorn's cup.
Clay records the cup's stippled cradle,
the clean border of its rim.

Smooth walls curve inwards
to a broken peak
where the squirrel tore
the oak's seed out of the ground.

I dig down through the ice of years
to feel the still-ragged scar
of my grandson's absence,
buried beneath layers of longing.

Suddenly Swans

Cloud, scummy as
an unwashed saucepan.
Lake-ice, robust bone.
Winter sticks to April.

Then, a swell of voices,
cheerful as children
released from school
to skip and shout at recess.

Voices surge from beyond the trees,
closer and closer and suddenly swans,
ribbons and ribbons of tundra swans.
They pelt over my head, low and loud,
long necks outstretched, until
my ears peal with their calls
my eyes startle at their rush, and
                         something buoyant springs.

A Woodland Healing

A twig of barbed wire
sprigs out of the trunk
of an aging maple
in these old farm woods.

The tree has grown
its phloem around the wire,
embedded sharp barbs
deep in the rings of its life.

Section IV

The Full Moon

"I stand alone under the fire of the great moon."
~Amy Lowell

Late News of My Grandfather, Percival Vincent Fright

Mother directs me to a frame, long tarnished
on her chest of drawers. Concealed behind it,
a creased letter, stained with age.

I open brittle folds to find a handsome script,
her father's hand, written from the trenches
of World War I to his seven-year-old daughter.

"Be a good girl, Joan," he wrote. "Take good care
of Mummy and baby Beryl and, above all else,
live your life with a clear conscience."

"How sad," I say. "He believed he would die
in France." "No, no!" insists Mother.
"That's not it at all. His conscience bothered him.

"He had someone else. They had a child,
you know. He kept two families,
so we were always pinched for money."

My gentle Grandpa! Elderly, as I remember him,
and married by then to Peggy, the Australian nurse
who had taken care of my dying grandmother.

"That Peggy Stringer!" sniffs Mother. When Grandpa died,
Peggy took the Fright silver teapot, the china tea set,
the scripts he illumined and the mantle clock to Australia.

As long as I can remember, my mother's lumbago,
her painful joints, were all male. When her right knee ground
and crackled, she'd say, "Damned Knee. He's bad today."

To explain trickling incontinence: "Bloomin' Tiddler,
he's always been unreliable." After she lost her breast,
she wept, "He was no good, and now he's gone."

Your Midnight Bed
Home, With My Mother

"Chick-ens," *you say, in your changed voice.*
Your side-slung mouth struggles: "Coop."
You want me to remember.
"The time you were locked in with the hens?"
Your eyes light as they used to.
"The time I came home from school?
I heard all this dreadful banging and shouting.
It came from the bottom of the garden."
One side of your mouth still remembers;
it twitches toward a smile.
"I thought it was the escaped lunatic,
the one from Banstead Asylum."
A rumble throbs in your throat.
"I even stepped outside by the coal bin.
The noise! Chickens squawking, shouts and thuds.
I ran inside and locked the back door,
certain the madman was chopping up
our chickens." *Your eyes blaze.*
"I opened the kitchen window. Shut it
and hid with my fingers in my ears."
You lie light with mirth in your midnight bed.
"Connie Smith heard and came to lift the fallen latch.
"Poor woman! She must have been terrified."
The sound in your throat explodes.
"You charged out, angry and stinking.
Chicken mess clung to your clothes, smeared
your hair and streaked your arms and skirt."
Your chest heaves with strange laughter.
"The hens didn't lay for three whole weeks."

Tears stream from your eyes, and I laugh, too,
in that complete way I learned from you.
I change and wash you in the sleeping house.
I arrange your limbs and tuck you in.
You nod toward your useless legs.
"Shut in," you mutter. "Again,"
your eyes, dull as pebbles.

On Tiptoe, I Listen

at her bedroom door.
No sound.

Maybe, in her sleep.
During the quiet of night,

my mother,
please let it be so.

I step, silent as breath,
into her darkened room,

morning tea in hand.
No movement.

I set down the china cup,
linger and look

at her diminished form,
curled like a winter leaf

beneath the woven wool coverlet.
I open heavy curtains

to see more clearly.
"What time is it, Liz?"

Relief surges,
warm as milk.

Impact

Where Dearborn crosses Superior,
a bundle of feathers,
crumpled in the gutter.
Pigeon, I think. But
this is as brown
as winter-seared leaves.
Three black bars
stripe a high-eyed head.
With my boot I tip it and see
a finger-length beak—
a woodcock
in the middle of Chicago!

Sheer walls of tinted glass reflect
high scudding clouds. I imagine
the woodcock's sure flight north,
distance and courtship in his breast,
singing wings fluting twilight air,
this ancient route imprinted
in his bones. It draws him
over plowed fields
and lonely farm houses,
wings beating, beating,
over small towns,
tracts of suburban houses,
factories, pluming black smoke,
into the canyons of packed city streets—
a sky of sudden glass.

The Snap of the Unseen

I set off for November woods the color of Irish tweed in a warm river of wind. Maples, oaks, and lindens rustle tawny gold and set leaves sifting to earth. A wash of milky light draws me out of close-woven woods and into open billows of tall-grass prairie. Spent seed heads of big bluestem brush my bare arms, feather my face. Newly arrived juncos swoop ahead of me, outer tail feathers flashing white. Robins flock southward. The dog tugs on, nose down, tail up, and I stride to keep his pace. Ahead, a thread of gossamer glints in low sun, some foolish spider, casting her silk into winter. The filament undulates, neither near, nor far. I duck to avoid it, and the dog hauls me forward; I feel a faint elastic strain across my cheek. Far away, my mother's heart falters. Early next morning the telephone jangles me awake. I hear my brother's hushed voice, know winter has come, snow-lined tree branches, my garden chair and yesterday's book, shrouded in white.

You Are the Upward in My Downward Years

When I arrive, you lie on a scale
in the glare of a bilirubin lamp.

A plastic peg clamps your cord.
Vernix waxes your elongated head.

You glow honey-pink. Tender. Asleep.
The nurse checks your skin and limbs,

turns you over, you, soft as a doll,
wraps you in cotton cloth

and sets you in my arms. You sleep
warm against my ribs. I admire

the almond curve of your tight-shut eyes,
the pressed furl of lips, precise

as the inner petal of an opening lotus—
my blood, my bones, my grand girl.

After My Mother Died

this bonsai pine, gnarled, lovely
but arrested, as she was by stroke,
worried me. I could no longer bear
its coffined existence. I prised it
out of its root-pinched dish, planted
it in a terracotta pot, five inches deep.

Imperceptibly, the pine stretches one limb
long as a sun-soothed cat,
and grows minute pollen cones. I kneel
to touch one—yellow bursts free, a brief
cloud of pollen gilds a slant of winter sun,
                              eddies and rises.

Leaving Eden

From her highchair, the baby watches me
set the knives and forks, pour water,
light the candle. I see frank wonder
at all the living around her. We sit
to eat. Her Uncle Fergus
puts his shabby cap on her head.
She touches the hat.

We laugh at the incongruity,
the large and the small, the worldly
and the innocent. She flaps her hands,
shakes her head, watches for response,
then flashes us a conscious smile.
I stroke the peach of her cheek
but regret this first small step
away from grace.

Perception

They descend to the Tuscan pool, exotic as bee-eaters,
two men, dark and lean, hair on chests and abdomens
glossy in sunlight, the young woman, slim as a Lombardy poplar.

Towels and a sheer wrap drop away. They plunge in,
swim, languid in cicáda-cradled heat. On aqua steps
they settle in the silvered shade of an olive tree

and murmur and laugh in Italian, voices as supple
as a conversation between Stradavari violins—
a Zeffirelli scene, and me, an on-the-set extra.

From behind my book, I admire them, a voyeur,
intent upon hiding my Anglo-Saxon clay. I conjure
purple figs in a shaded courtyard, a laden table,

Ferragamo shoes, talk of La Scala and Berlusconi.
The taller man says, "So, I took out his second molar,"
in the angled twang of Chicago. I set down my book,

dive in, shatter surface dazzle.

I Watch a Least Tern Fishing
On Amy's Third Broken Engagement

Butterfly-bird, you flitter above
life's shifting estuary, tail forked,
head and yellow beak down, alert
to the fickle fin-flick of silver.

You fold wings, plummet
headlong, like a girl falling
in love, slick as an arrow,
ease from much practice.

No catch. You struggle out
and up; five heavy wingbeats
and you shiver off failure, scatter
droplets, bright as tears.

The Smell of Apples

Crab apples molder, thick as blood,
beneath our tree, the time of year
my mother used to come and stay.

In the heady scent of rot
she taught me how to make
apple glaze and Bakewell tarts;

I helped her bathe and dress.
Together we argued, talked and read
through the vinegar-sweet days.

She asked to stay in Minnesota,
far from England, but with me,
her only daughter. I wanted

to keep her, wanted to nurse
her slow decline, but we could not
afford insurance for a failing English heart.

I had to send her home to die.
Now, in September, the tang
of fermenting apple flesh

trips a deep, familiar ache.
Thirsty for my mother,
I gulp the cider air.

Waiting for the Bear

A shadow with shoulders,
it lumbers from the woods.

It is pure darkness, fur
so dense, it swallows light.

How I long for and dread
the honey-tongued,

berry-eating, heavy sleeper;
rooter beneath

overturned rocks, revealer
of old putrefactions.

Come, stir your unpredictable bulk.
Let me hear the rustle

of your tread on leaf duff—
feel your breath, urgent

on my neck. Come, startle me.
Shamble onto my frightened page.

Section V

The Waning Quarter Moon

"The Moon understands what it is to be human.
Uncertain. Alone. Cratered by imperfections."
~Tahereh Mafi

Pointe du Hoc, Normandy

Omaha Beach lies west. Utah stretches east.
A farmer blades dark weals into damp earth.
White gulls glide in the plow's slow wake.
Beyond a bramble hedge, a cow, square
as a Panzer tank, chews her cud.

A sea-wind chills me at the cliff's edge.
I think of our two American sons.

On this cliff-top, young Americans
knocked out a six-gun German battery
embedded in steel and concrete.
An Atlantic storm pounded high seas
into the swollen Channel. Landing vessels
blew off course. Some sank. Young men
crabbed over sea-slammed rocks, scrambled
up the cliff's tall jut. Support fire hurtled above,
German grenades exploding around them.
Injured boys fell to the rocks below.
Survivors climbed on. They took
the promontory and held it, tearing metal
ahead, the sheer drop behind.

At my feet, two field poppies, petals
still crumpled from the bud's tight pack,
shiver in the salty updraft,
fragile crimson tissue.

Where She Hid

Prinsengracht Straat, Amsterdam

I listen to the sounds of morning
as Anne must have listened from the blind
windows of her stale attic: the call of a magpie
scissors still air; a bristle broom scratches
over cobbles; two bicycles creak past,
one pedal knocking the mudguard,
its bang bulleting down the narrow
canyon of this old Dutch street.

A sudden carillon of church bells.
On the street below Anne's hushed attic,
I hear young voices. Through the limbs
of a budding chestnut, I glimpse girls
chattering as they walk to school.
An early sun rises at their backs;
their shadows stretch ahead of them,
long as the promise of their fresh young lives.

I Stop Writing the Poem

to water my sagging Christmas cactus, to
bring in damp wash when it starts to spit, to
answer the phone. It's my daughter-in-law
in England, asking me to look up
her doctor's telephone number
and to mail her a Cambodian alphabet book.

I pick up my pencil, to retrace my thoughts
when
FedEx knocks, with a package; he wants a signature.
The dog barks and leaps.
The FedEx man reminds me to clean leaf-packed gutters.

The dog whines to be let out. I empty
trash at the same time, take out recycling,
pick white Evening Star roses
before the freeze tonight—glimpse an owl
drop out of the twilight.

I race to find binoculars,
watch the owl mantle wide wings
for balance—
some small thing, dying,
down in the clutter.

It's a matter of time.

Terezin

On Visiting a Nazi Holding Camp in Czech Republic

Above the iron gate, "Arbeit Macht Frei."
Like those before, we walk beneath the lie,
Ken, Vashek, Vlosda, and little Kuba.
We pass the bare washroom, built to impress
credulous inspectors from the Red Cross,
see sheds for forced labor; punishment cells.
We walk through blocks stacked with bunks—
ghosts of fathers, separated mothers,
children shipped away, early, to the east.

We step over weed-choked railroad tracks
to a crescent of uncut grasses. Kuba
drops his mother's hand and skips
ahead to a hillock of wild flowers.
We watch him gather ox-eye daisies
until his hands are full. "Dada," he calls,
holding up his bouquet. Vashek hesitates,
caught in the past, then drops to one knee
and knots the stems with a stalk
of reed-canary grass. Kuba runs
to give his mother the present.

Origins

For My Friend, Thach In

Because you left your country behind
Because you had to flee the Khmer Rouge
        and escape to a Thai refugee camp
        to save your children
Because you left your language behind
        your temple and heaps of bleached skulls
Because you left behind your mother
        in your village, on its stilts, and she waited
        for you to come up the river on the day
        each year, when Tonle Sap reverses its flow
        and she watched for you, until the day she died
Because a part of you lives among mangos, monks, buffalo and silks
        heat, jack fruit, lotus and sweet-water fish
        sesame, blessings, laughter and vanished family
        you are a reed, ripped in two
      bending in a river that flows backwards
every year, yearning to find its source.

Flight
9-11-2001

A swallow swoops
through insect-fat air, flight effortless—
irrational summer exuberance.

A falcon strikes an unsuspecting pigeon,
exploding it in a burst
of September feathers.

Migrating white pelicans,
robust as B 2 bombers, heave
into the air from a steel-gray lake.

Flights of high tundra swans
ghost through a ground-glass sky,
whispering, "Winter."

I Cut a White Onion

With knife tip, I flick on the kitchen radio.
Sienna outer skin shells free.
Tough under-layers cling tight. I cut off
the top and dried root ends, catch
coarse layers between knife and thumb
and tear them off—*In Dialo Province,*
an IED peeled back the protective plating
on a Humvee, killing four soldiers . . .
Stripped, the onion lies sleek
on my yellow-wood board.

My fingers curl around layered symmetry,
sense in the firm onion flesh the potential
to live and grow. Right hand, deft
and quick, takes the Sabatier blade,
slices the onion from bud to bottom.
I cannot escape its burst of sap—
Twenty-one bodies of tortured Iraqi police,
throats cut, were unearthed earlier today . . .
I feel my nostrils prickle, eyes tear.
My knife severs compact tissue
lengthwise, then crosswise.

I drop a test piece into the pan.
Hot oil leaps to sear onion in sizzle.
I tilt the chopping board, slide
onion-chips into ready oil—*A suicide bomber*
exploded his charge in a crowded market
in Karbala. Charred remains litter the . . .
I snap off the radio, turn off the heat,
appetite gone—a cut onion, wet eyes,
and silence.
This capable knife, sharp in my hand.

How to Let Light into the Soul

Predators don't chat.
The doe stamps and snorts,
flight a mere hair-flick away.
I stand statue-still. *Predators*
creep, stealthy and silent.
She lowers her alarm flag.
An anxious fawn peers
from beneath her belly.
Talkers are harmless.
Another doe eases
from between tree trunks,
her fawn, bold. He stamps,
takes two steps toward me.
If you don't mind, I'll sit down.
I move, slow as a katydid,
to a fallen maple limb.
He skitters back to Mother.
White tails flare. Then settle.
We share much of our DNA, after all.
Each doe nudges nearer.
A third deer and new fawn,
coat still mottled, enter our circle.
It's all about love and trust.
Sounds of the outside world
drop away. I belong on my log,
stilled by the curiosity of woodland kin.

Step by cautious step,
the older fawn draws closer,
damp nose extended,
nostrils flared, under-chin, white,
tense ears, dark-rimmed,
blond hairs within,
until I feel his breath
warm on my knees—

I long to touch the sleek
stretch of his neck,
fingers ready to leaf . . .

At Gate C38, Denver Airport

An airport security van waits, lights flashing.
A polished black hearse draws close, maneuvers
until its double back doors face the airplane.
An immaculately clad marine swings open rear doors,
wide arms, ready to welcome a loved one home.
More white hats, bright in mile-high sun,
brass buttons glinting, taut bellies tight,
backs straight as young timber. A stretch limousine
glides to a halt. A soldier steps to its door. A woman,
heavy, in blue jeans, climbs out; her husband,
crumpled parka unzipped; a teenage son, hands
pushed into pockets. They wait, awkward,
each turned from the other. A white-gloved officer
snaps a salute. Chins lift. Six marines in dress uniform
bear a coffin draped in Stars and Stripes. They process,
slowly, to the open hearse. The coffin slides in.
Doors close. Husband and son return to the limousine.
She stands, locked in the tomb of this moment.
                    The officer touches her arm.

The Daily Smallness of Being

My neighbor, reliable as sunrise, forgets
to remember, and two brothers call to tell me,
breaths catching, they have cancer.
My friend of twenty-eight years dies.
Our warming planet spawns hurricanes, floods,
and drought. Ice caps calve. Counties burn.
An ill-chosen war unites an ideology against us.
Unease silts in the blood and does not leave.

Only in the daily smallness of being
lies an immense pleasure in living: the ruby fire
of a hummingbird's throat as he threatens me,
my car keys where they should be,
gray friction of pencil on paper;
a pan-hot, parmesan omelette,
the smell of sunlight on my night pillow,
the sandpaper-rub of a day's end beard.

In My Kitchen Cupboard I Keep

a tin of Tate and Lyle's Golden Syrup,
unused but necessary for me to know it's there.
On its label, bees hive in the cave of a dead lion's ribs,
its caption, "Out of the strong came forth sweetness,"
like Britain's rule over a quarter of the globe.
As children, we argued about how truly sweet
honey could be when nested in the chest of death;

I keep my childhood in a confident nation,
natives living under British rule in the many
pink-colored countries of our school atlases,
our justice a beacon, shining forth in dark lands.
I store the gift of the English language,
the art of conversation over tea and tiffin,
Caribbean sugar cane, Malayan nutmeg,
Maltese capers, Burmese pepper,
condiments and colonized subcontinents,
spices, gold, tea, diamonds, coffee, oil,
roads and railways, built on the sands
of divide and rule, Great Britain, great
purveyor of goods to the world.

I keep a bottle of sweetened Camp Coffee concentrate,
so old it has evaporation marks down its length,
tree rings, marking my long years away. On its label,
a mustachioed officer in a kilt sits on a military drum
under India's blazing sun and sips coffee
from a china cup, turbaned servant at his side,
India, Kashmir, Pakistan, Burma, Uganda,
Kenya, Iraq, our legacy, a list of troubled nations.

I keep my bottle of Camp Coffee, lid
rusted to the neck of lost conviction.

Sudden Inundation Is a Necessary Condition

Encyclopedia Britannica, "Fossil"

then time does its work. Minerals seep
into bones over millennia, until the whole
becomes stone, with the form of what was,
but is no longer the original. America
is changing me, without my consent.

How Sweet the Silence of Lemons

San Dominico, Taormina, Sicily

Idle as a moth in daytime, I pluck and peel a blood orange
from a gnarled branch, juice sticky on my fingers,
tartness sharp on my tongue. Freesia-scented air. Hot sun.

A metal-green gecko basks on the hip of a terracotta urn.
For centuries in this high garden, monks toiled to grow
fruits and vegetables for their Dominican brothers.

Bees hum in a bed of calendula. Far below, the Mediterranean
washes and ebbs, and the constant ache of war-news fades.
Here, no roads explode; no gun-ships roam the air.

A linnet preens on the twig end of an espaliered peach.
Time and aloneness. Distant Mount Etna puffs gently,
and peace trellises the mind, tendril by tender tendril.

Section VI

The Fading Crescent Moon

"Gray hairs seem to my fancy like the soft light of the moon,
silvering over the evening of life."
~Jean Paul

New Neighbors

Alien ladybugs swarm orange
under russet maples, bump
into my book, bite my bare arms.
Dry and warm. Late October.
Shouting crows harass an owl
in the great white oak.
Traffic hurtles overhead to the airport.
Snarl of a chainsaw. It idles,
close, but out of view.
I hear it engage wood,
gnaw and fuss and grind.

Silence.

A creak.

My sky

                        explodes open.

My garden chair
quakes.

They've cut down
the white oak.
I stare into its

                    sky hole

In the Brimming Bowl of My Head

I can open the back door to childhood,
step into our kitchen and smell
that our mum has been ironing dry
a damp English wash, the room
filled with tired heat and hard-pressed folds.

The old refrigerator purrs quietly,
Danny the cat poured across its shoulders,
the anthracite boiler, warm in its corner,
our dog, Tina, sprawled before it,
paws flicking in dreamed chase.

I can walk through rooms still undivided
by cheap wallboard, loved spaces,
run up the stairs, past the stained-glass window,
into the bathroom, where my startled father's
huge nakedness once shocked me;

past my brothers' room, a glance into
my own and dreams of Norman Walker's
full lips, on to our parents' bedroom,
their separate beds adrift
on a long-gone sea of pale blue carpet.

I can duck into the lounge, see
its paned windows, generous French doors
swung wide to the summer night and tea roses,
Tchaikovsky's "Pathetique" grieving
on the turntable, my father in his chair,

a burning point of light in the tobacco dark of memory.

To an Unpracticed Eye

In Oxford's urban gardens,
spires of bluebells grow tall and sturdy,
wildflowers reclaiming their native soil,
where centuries ago had grown virgin stands
of oak, elm and chestnut. I, too, am returned,
joyful to be in England in springtime.

A friend tells me, these pale spires
are imported bluebells, foreign spreaders.
To an unpracticed eye, they are the real thing.

I find true English bluebells at Kew,
each short stem bowed in a curve of bells,
their color, intense indigo. To some, I might appear
true British, but I have paled in long years away, grown
strong and straight with acquired American directness.
I am an import in my native land.

Baking in the Kitchen on a Gray Morning

I barely notice at first,
a black dab on new snow
beneath the bird feeder,
the brutal cold, a gray bird,
perched in the sapling ash.

I press shortbread dough
into a fluted ceramic dish
and the bird swoops to savage
the small creature—
a Northern shrike, tossing its prey.

I see a short tail, a shrew snout,
blood, bright on snow,
one hind leg scrabbling,
see the bird fly, heavy,
shrew clasped in claws.

I think about the unexpected, how it
can come from within, cancer cells
colonizing the continent of the body,
the rogue clot, free and seeking its fortune
in the narrow streets of the heart.

Death, hidden and silent; or perched
and alert, hooked beak ready.
Sudden sun fractures rainbow prisms
through a cut-glass vase, and my kitchen
blazes with the present—

five clementines flame impossibly orange
against winter's brilliant rug of white,
but the voice of the slate clock
claims my ears, its two hands
gathering in the hours.

You've Got to Love a Man Who Cares Enough to Stop and Kill

A car-struck sparrow thrashes
on a narrow Donegal road,

flutters and spins, too broken
to live, not broken enough to die.

David brakes and backs up,
fuchsia hedgerow scratching metal.

A car tears by; its momentum
sets the fuchsia opposite, bucking.

Behind, a bread van hoots. David
waves him past, backs further,

aims his right tire and inches forward.
He pulls into the hedgerow to check.

His wheel aim was true, the sparrow,
a crush of still feathers.

He puts the van into gear and says,
"Hope we don't find a hit sheep."

Two Snakes Twined in Bridal Veil

That part of the brain that registers but does not record,
notes a thickening of twigs in the bridal veil. I peg
pajamas on the washing line, fingers chilled. Hoarfrost
rimes the grass, but the radio promises sixty degrees.

I hang up pillowcases, look again, see a garter snake,
long and looped, sinews wrapped around vines,
charcoal stripes and orange flecks along a flowing flank,
narrow head, stilled by cold, immobile as carved wood.

Sheets swell in awakening air. I look closer,
see a second head, two silky lengths coiled as one
for warmth, tails twisted in double-ply, like love,
like our two lives, twined by time and common comfort.

In My November Mirror, My Mother's Face

I still wear my mother's shoes,
Clark's sandals, flat and practical.
She limped to the Bexhill shops
through damp English summers,
stamping discontent into her tread,
her life cramped by two world wars,
a hunger for things she couldn't afford.

I have an easier life, born to better times,
but I yearn to find that lost path home
to a distant Bexhill of the soul.
Clasped in her sandals' close embrace,
I pace a trodden road; her lameness scuffed
the right heel low, mine shallows the left,
as I walk towards my mother in my mother's shoes.

A Snail Paints Glaze Along My Arm

I lie flat in November woods.
Bare branches bow skywards.

The ground rustles around me.
Fingers root in loam.

Damp seeps into bones,
skin sheds into leaf litter.

Time is the worm,
night the filament.

Moss gathers on
the log of my leg.

I pull close
Earth's mantle,

mottle
in its soft embrace.

I Always Eat an Apple Whole

The flesh, core, and polished brown seeds
all go down. I chomp until just the stem
remains, pinched between index and thumb.
People ask me why? Because I grew up
during the war, I tell them, when food
was scarce; but really it's because I like
to chew, like the core's toenail snag
between my teeth, the unexpected truth
of bitter almond in the pips. I like
poetry, where disquiet lurks, hidden
deep inside its outward form, stories
that are crisp and unexpected. I like
life tart and succulent, scarred and real.